SO YOU WANNA BE A Writer

K.A. ROBERTSON

Rourke Educational Media

rourkeeducationalmedia.com

Before & After Reading Activities

Before Reading:

Building Academic Vocabulary and Background Knowledge

Before reading a book, it is important to tap into what your child or students already know about the topic. This will help them develop their vocabulary, increase their reading comprehension, and make connections across the curriculum.

1. Look at the cover of the book. What will this book be about?
2. What do you already know about the topic?
3. Let's study the Table of Contents. What will you learn about in the book's chapters?
4. What would you like to learn about this topic? Do you think you might learn about it from this book? Why or why not?
5. Use a reading journal to write about your knowledge of this topic. Record what you already know about the topic and what you hope to learn about the topic.
6. Read the book.
7. In your reading journal, record what you learned about the topic and your response to the book.
8. After reading the book complete the activities below.

Content Area Vocabulary

Read the list. What do these words mean?

acquire
collaborate
critique
deadlines
dialogue
fiction
freelance
intern
pitch
reputable
vet

After Reading:

Comprehension and Extension Activity

After reading the book, work on the following questions with your child or students in order to check their level of reading comprehension and content mastery.

1. What do technical writers do? (Summarize)
2. Why is it important to read a lot if you want to be a good writer? (Infer)
3. What is the goal of copywriting? (Asking Questions)
4. How do your favorite books influence your writing style? (Text to Self Connection)
5. What specialties do content writers need to be familiar with? (Asking Questions)

Extension Activity

Start keeping an observation notebook with you at all times. Write down interesting things you see or hear. Write about the way things make you feel, or how an experience changed your thinking. Take notes on funny or interesting conversations you have or overhear. You will soon have a notebook full of material you can use to inspire stories, shape characters, and develop plots. You can also use your notes to inspire your nonfiction writing. The things that catch your attention now can give you new ideas in the future!

Table of Contents

Write On!..................................4
Newspapers, Magazines,
    and Blogs............................6
Writing for Businesses
    and Organizations................14
Creative Writers......................20
Glossary................................30
Index....................................31
Show What You Know..............31
Further Reading.....................31
About the Author...................32

Write On!

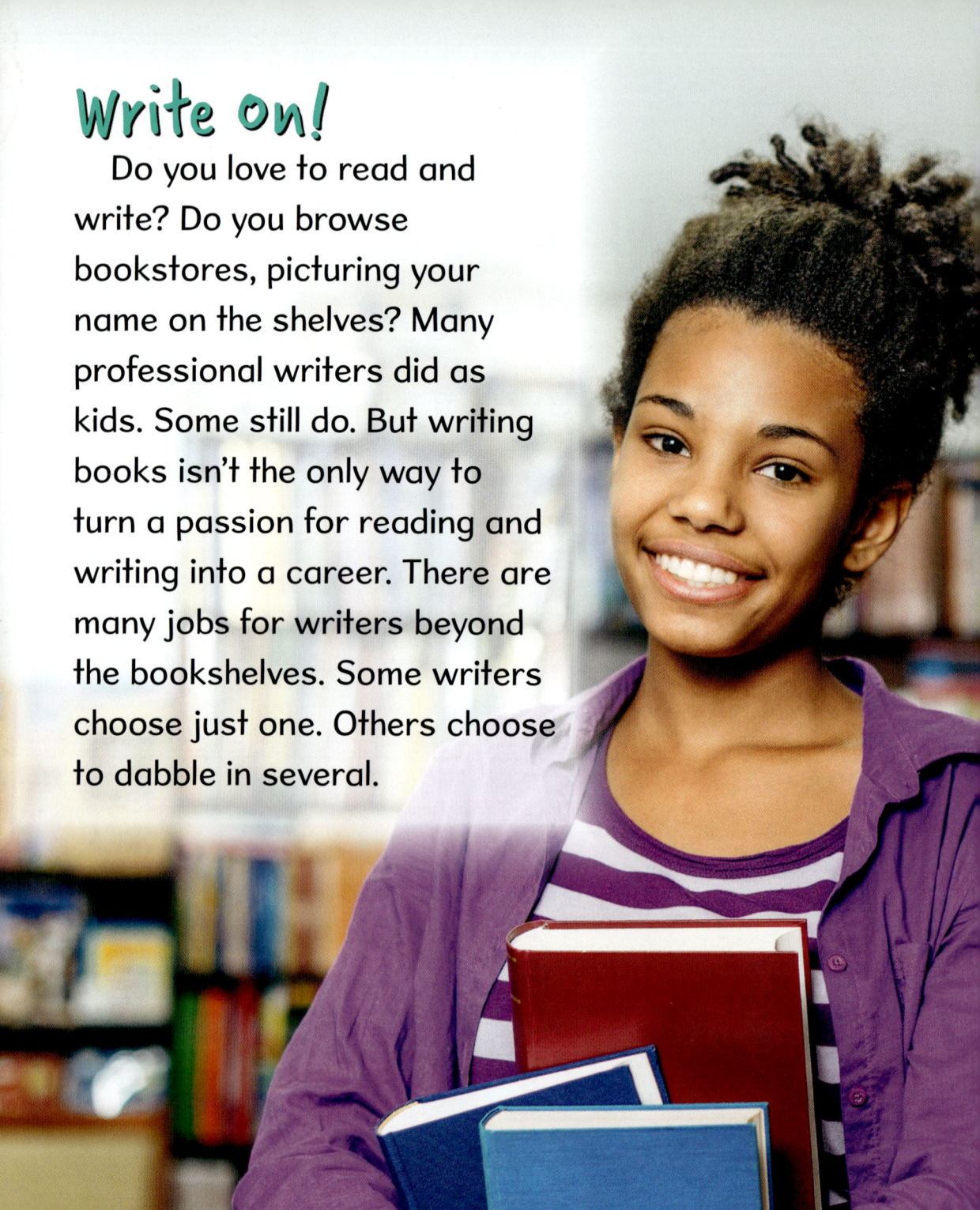

Do you love to read and write? Do you browse bookstores, picturing your name on the shelves? Many professional writers did as kids. Some still do. But writing books isn't the only way to turn a passion for reading and writing into a career. There are many jobs for writers beyond the bookshelves. Some writers choose just one. Others choose to dabble in several.

WORKING WITH WORDS

"The only kind of writing is rewriting," Ernest Hemingway said. A first draft is rarely good, much less great. Writers often go through many revisions to get to a final draft.

Newspapers, Magazines, and Blogs

Print Journalists

Print journalists write for newspapers, magazines, and news websites. They write about everything from wars to weddings. Some journalists choose a specialty, such as sports, entertainment, or politics. Some write opinion columns. Others are reporters who cover general news.

A journalist typically does research, conducts interviews, and writes articles quickly to meet **deadlines**. As each article is published, their collection of clips, or published works, grows. Their clips can help them pursue other types of writing jobs.

Ready to get started? Write for your school newspaper. Don't have one? Start one! Tools such as the free interactive printing press at www.readwritethink.org can help you create it.

PRO ADVICE

"Start by reading books, magazines, and newspapers. See how words paint pictures. Write a blog, diary, short stories, anything. Find something extraordinary in everyday life and describe it. Never let anyone tell you no. A teacher told me I wasn't serious enough about journalism to be on my high school paper. I proved her wrong." — Joe Henderson, journalist with more than 45 years of experience

7

Journalists work with editors to develop stories. An editor may assign a story, or writers may **pitch** stories for approval. To write for a newspaper or magazine, writers often need a degree in journalism or mass communication.

DID YOU KNOW?!
All reporters are journalists. But not all journalists are reporters. Reporters gather and write facts about newsworthy events. Journalists include opinion columnists and editorial writers whose writing includes analysis and opinion based on news reports.

Interns at The New York Times learn the news and business side of journalism.

GIGS FOR KIDS

Time for Kids accepts applications for student reporters every year. Check out www.timeforkids.com for information on becoming one of Time's kid journalists!

College students can **intern** at a publication for experience. Interning also introduces them to people in the business. Knowing people in the business is important! Making connections is a big part of finding writing jobs. Some writers are employed by one publication. Others **freelance** and write for several publications.

Bloggers

Anyone can start a blog. You can start writing your own blog today! Blogs are websites that are regularly updated with new content. Some blogs focus on a single topic, such as world news, community events, or cooking. Others cover several topics, much like a news website.

Writers can find paying jobs writing for popular blogs. They can also start their own blogs and earn money from advertisements. You don't always need a college degree to write for blogs. You do need to have a collection of clips to show blog editors you can write well.

FAST FACTS
Blogs make money from advertisers and sometimes product promotion. Popular blogs attract advertisers that want to reach the blog's audience.

Bloggers often rely on social media to share their stories and bring readers to their websites.

Some bloggers used to be journalists. Some bloggers were not. Journalists are trained to **vet** sources, report facts, and make it clear to readers when a story is opinion, not fact. **Reputable** publications require writers to follow these standards. Blogs do not always follow these rules. They may quote unreliable sources or report half-truths. If you want to start a blog, you should follow journalistic standards to avoid producing what's called "fake news."

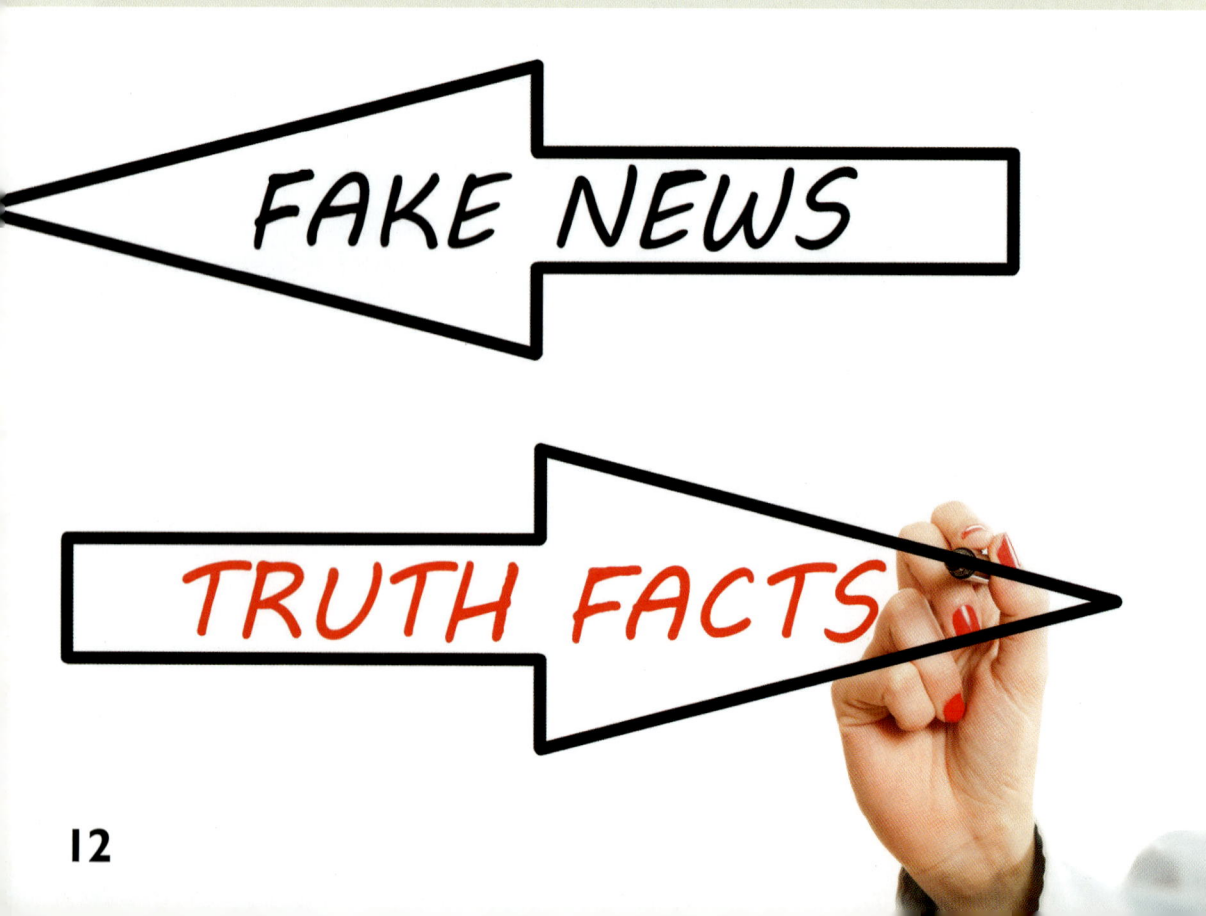

Feature Stories

Feature stories are popular in newspapers, magazines, and online. These stories can also provide inspiration for **fiction** writers' stories. Types of features include:

Human interest: A police officer buys groceries for a shoplifter. A couple skydives to celebrate their 60th wedding anniversary. A man wins a marathon after losing a leg. Human interest features tell the emotional stories of people and their concerns or achievements.

Informational: These features provide practical, social, or historical information. A story about a town's history, a how-to article on car repair, and an article about an upcoming event are examples of informational features.

Profiles: These stories are based on interviews with an individual. They give the reader insight into a person's personality, interests, and opinions or views.

Travel: Travel features tell readers about a place the writer visited and their experiences there. These include the writer's opinion about things such as hotels, entertainment, and restaurants.

Writing for Businesses and Organizations

Copywriters write text, called copy, for businesses and other organizations. The goal of their writing is to get people to take an action. Copywriters do research and conduct interviews to produce copy, often for multiple clients at once. They must write in a way that reflects the client's tone, or voice, rather than their own.

FAST FACT

Industries that employ copywriters include:
- Banks
- Insurance agencies
- Tech companies
- Manufacturers
- Government agencies
- Healthcare organizations
- Publishers
- Political organizations

Copywriters may work for a copywriting agency that serves many clients. Others may work for a single business.

Content Writers

Imagine this: You want to learn how to play the guitar. You search "How to Play Guitar" online. The first search result: Learn to Play Guitar in Three Easy Steps! You click on it and read. Then you notice the website belongs to a business that sells guitars and guitar lessons. They didn't reach you with an advertisement. You came to them because they gave you information. Content writers specialize in creating content that brings potential customers to business websites.

Content writers often have degrees in English or journalism. And they aren't just good writers. Because the goal of their work is to increase web traffic, they also must be social media and SEO savvy.

DID YOU KNOW?!
SEO stands for Search Engine Optimization. SEO is a collection of techniques such as keyword placement that increase traffic to a website. The goal of SEO is to make a website come up among the top results in a search engine for one or more topics.

Business Writers

Business writers often work as freelancers for multiple clients. Their projects may include resumes, reports, employee biographies, company newsletters, press releases, and business plans. These writers often do research and conduct interviews to create materials for their clients.

Freelance business writers are entrepreneurs. Like other freelancers, they operate as a business themselves. They use websites, social media, and networking to promote their services and get new clients.

Grant Writers

Private and public foundations award grant money for specific projects or causes. Grant writers research, write, and submit proposals for individuals or organizations applying for these grants. Some grant writers work full time for charities or nonprofit organizations. Some work as freelancers writing grant proposals for multiple clients in a variety of areas, from medical research to museums.

PRO ADVICE

"Grant writing is not much different from the research papers you write for school! It's all about following instructions, properly citing your references, and making a strong case. Learn to love your English class, and read as much as you can!" —Rebecca Sitten, professional grant writer

Grant writers use their research skills to search for grants that match their clients' projects.

FAST FACT:
Grant and textbook writers often have degrees in English, creative writing, communication, marketing, or journalism. Textbook writers may also have degrees in the subjects they write about.

Textbook Writers

All kinds of schools use textbooks, from kindergarten to college! Businesses and training programs use them too. Textbook writers have great writing skills and expert knowledge in the subjects they write about.

Technical Writers

Have you ever read instructions for playing a video game or using an appliance? That's the work of a technical writer! Technical writers make complex information easier to understand. A technical writer may write about legal policies. Or they may write instructions for using a product such as computer software.

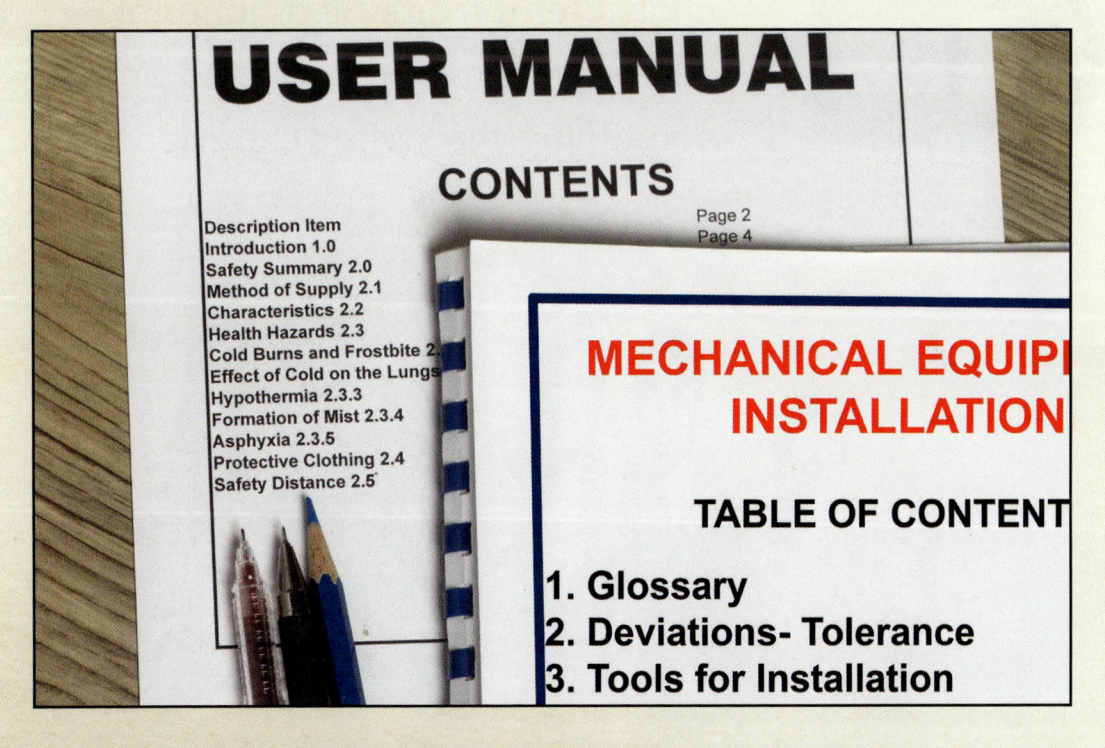

Technical writing jobs often require a bachelor's degree. Some schools offer technical writing programs.

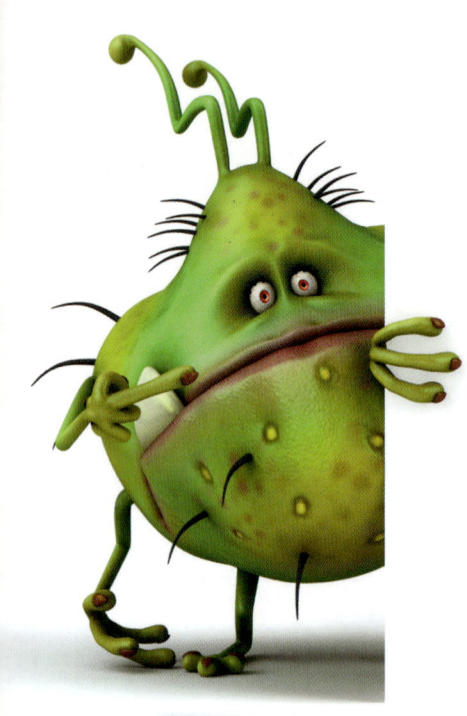

Creative Writers

The writing careers we've touched on so far deal in facts. Ready to ditch reality? Creative writers make things up! Sometimes they get a little help from real life, though. Fiction writers are often inspired by their real-world experiences and observations. A character's traits or a fictional conversation may be based on something the writer experienced.

TV and Movies

Next time you're watching your favorite TV show or movie, note what you like about it. Is it the suspense? The funny **dialogue**? Whatever hooks you, a writer or team of writers is likely responsible for it. From comedies to dramas to late-night talk shows, writers craft much of what you see and hear.

Television writers create the plots, characters, situations, and dialogue for TV shows. Screenwriters do the same for movies.

TV writers and screenwriters don't need a specific degree. Some take television writing or screenwriting courses to develop their skills. Like other writing jobs, networking helps people make connections and find jobs.

SCREENWRITING COMPETITION!
ENTER

WRITE NOW!
A search online turns up several screenwriting competitions for kids. With your teacher or parents' help, you can find reputable competitions in which to submit your work.

Want to write for TV or film? Start by being observant. Watch people interact. Take notes on funny or interesting things you see or hear. Use your experiences to create stories.

DID YOU KNOW?!
You can use a website such as www.storyboardthat.com to create a storyboard for a TV or movie script. Try coming up with your own script for the characters in your favorite TV show. Put them in a situation you haven't seen them in. What will they say and do?

★ ★ PRO ADVICE ★ ★

"If you want to be a TV writer, you should start by watching TV. (Tell your parents you're doing research for your future career!) Pay attention to your favorite shows. What do you like about them? What kinds of stories are you most drawn to? What makes you root for a certain character? Dissecting your favorite TV shows to figure out what makes them work is a great starting point for honing your craft. You should also read and write as much as possible to begin finding your own voice."
—Joanna Quraishi, professional TV writer

Publishing Contract

Writing Books

Book authors write fiction, nonfiction, or both. They may write for kids, teens, adults, or every age. Like TV writers and screenwriters, they often use their experiences and observations in their work.

Some authors develop an idea, write a book, then submit it to publishers in hopes one will **acquire** it. Others are hired to write books based on a publisher's idea.

> **FAST FACT**
> The Writer's Market is published every year. This giant book includes information about what publishers and agents are looking for. It's a great tool for getting to know about the industry.

AGENTS
Many book publishers and production companies only work with writers represented by an agent. Getting the right agent requires research. But only after you've written the best book or script possible! Agents want to represent writers whose work they feel strongly about bringing to an audience.

Becoming a published author requires getting to know the industry and the people who work in it. Networking is important, especially for new authors. They often attend writing workshops and conferences with professional editors and agents to make contacts and get their work noticed.

Book authors don't need college degrees to be published. But they do need strong writing skills. They also need to work well with others, especially their editors. A book often goes through many rounds of edits before the publisher approves it. This process can be difficult for an author who is not open to **critique** or compromise.

> **DID YOU KNOW?!**
> Some popular book series are written by several authors writing under a single name. These ghostwriters are given a contract and outlines to follow in developing the books for the series.

She was born in P... deformed. This was not a great s... many dis abled persons suffer great unwanted by their families. In fac feeling ~~chamed~~ *shamed* by his daughter's Unfortunately, her mother ... She had to ~~live~~ *leave* s...

26

PRO ADVICE

"If you want to be a writer, you should:
1. Read adventurously and deeply. Read everything and anything that sparks your interest. And then if it's good, read it again and figure out how it works, and why it works.
2. Write every day, in the same location and time. Half an hour a day is a good amount of time to start. What you are doing is developing a writing habit. After a while, you may not be able to sleep if you haven't written. Write about anything. Experiment. Write about the everyday world. Describe people coming into rooms. Describe a flash of the eyes, the sun in the trees. Get into the habit of making art.
3. Live a life that's worth writing about. Be interesting, courageous, and passionate. If your life is all those things, then your writing will be all those things as well.
4. Don't procrastinate. Get started now! Go fast, but take your time."

—Theo Baker, author

Writing Songs

What's your favorite song? What story does it tell? Songwriters write lyrics and melodies for music. Lyricists just write lyrics. These writers work with music publishers, recording artists, and record producers to create new songs. Some write alone, others **collaborate** with other writers. They may spend their days writing, attending meetings, or recording song demos.

You don't need a degree to become a songwriter or lyricist. But songwriting classes can help sharpen your skills.

Hit songwriters can make millions. But only a few reach this level. Many work day jobs and write songs on the side.

The notes you take now may become part of a book or song you write years from now.

"Most of the basic material a writer works with is acquired before the age of fifteen," acclaimed author Willa Cather once said. Observe the world and the people in it. Take notes. Read lots! Listen to music. Pay attention to the lyrics. Explore your interests. Find new interests! Learn new words. Experiment with different styles of writing. And try to write at least a little every day.

Glossary

acquire (uh-KWIRE): to get something so you own or have it

collaborate (kuh-LAB-uh-rate): work together to do something

critique (KRIT-eek): a critical analysis of a written work

deadlines (DED-lines): times when things must be finished

dialogue (DYE-uh-lawg): conversation, especially in a book, play, movie, or TV show

fiction (FIK-shuhn): stories about characters and events that are not real

freelance (FREE-lans): freelance workers get paid for individual jobs completed, and may work for various companies

intern (IN-turn): someone who is learning a skill or job by working with an expert in that field

pitch (pich): a talk or presentation meant to persuade you to do something

reputable (REP-yuh-tuh-buhl): having a good reputation; trustworthy

vet (vet): make a careful, critical examination of something

Index

author(s) 24, 25, 26, 29
blog(s) 7, 10, 11, 12
content 10, 15
copywriters 14
creative 18, 20
film 22
grant(s) 17
journalist(s) 6, 7, 8, 9, 12
movie(s) 21, 22
songwriter(s) 28
technical 19
textbook(s) 18
TV 21, 22, 23, 24

Show What You Know

1. What does a copywriter do?
2. What types of college degrees are helpful for writers?
3. How can watching TV help you prepare for a writing career?
4. What is networking and why is it important?
5. What does an agent do for writers?

Further Reading

Mahoney, Ellen, *Nellie Bly and Investigative Journalism for Kids: Mighty Muckrakers from the Golden Age to Today*, Chicago Review Press, 2015.

Mazer, Anne, *Spilling Ink: A Young Writer's Handbook*, Square Fish, 2010.

Stowell, Louie, *Write Your Own Story Book*, Usborne Books, 2011.

About the Author

K.A. Robertson decided she wanted to be a writer when a story she wrote in the fourth grade was bound into a book and put in the school library. She has a bachelor's degree in English and a master's degree in mass communications. K.A. has worked as a journalist, content writer, business writer, and book author.

Meet The Author!
www.meetREMauthors.com

© 2019 Rourke Educational Media

All rights reserved. No part of this book may be reproduced or utilized in any form or by any means, electronic or mechanical including photocopying, recording, or by any information storage and retrieval system without permission in writing from the publisher.

www.rourkeeducationalmedia.com

PHOTO CREDITS: Cover & Title Pg ©CatLane, Pg 7, 17, 23, 27 ©MariatKary, Pg 3, 14, top bar ©thawornnurak, Pg 4 Drazen Lovric, Pg 7 By Niloo, Pg 8 mizoula, Pg 9 By Ollyy, Pg 10 By Kaspars Grinvalds, Pg 11 ArtemSam, By BigTunaOnline, Pg 12 marrio31, Pg 14 pixelfit, Pg 15 LightFieldStudios, Pg 16 mediaphotos, Pg 17 By Tashatuvango, Pg 18 beaucroft, Pg 19 By RAGMA IMAGES, Pg 20 julos, krisanapong detraphiphat, Pg 21 krisanapong detraphiphat, ©fad1986, Pg 22 finwal, Pg 23 YinYang, Joanna Quarashi, Pg 24 alexskopje, Pg 25 ferrantraite, Pg 26 & 27 ©By Lamai Prasitsuwan, Pg 28 santypan, Pg 29 pepifoto,

Edited by: Keli Sipperley
Cover and Interior design by: Rhea Magaro-Wallace

Library of Congress PCN Data

A Writer / K.A. Robertson
 (So You Wanna Be)
 ISBN 978-1-64156-473-1 (hard cover)
 ISBN 978-1-64156-599-8 (soft cover)
 ISBN 978-1-64156-714-5 (e-Book)
Library of Congress Control Number: 2018930509

Rourke Educational Media
Printed in the United States of America,
North Mankato, Minnesota

WEIRD, TRUE FACTS

MONSTERS

K.A. Robertson

Rourke Educational Media
rourkeeducationalmedia.com

World Monster Map

Canada
North America
Haiti
Puerto Rico
Loch Ness
Transylvania
Africa
Mount Everest
Australia

Monster myths come from all parts of the world. There are land monsters, sea monsters, and flying monsters! Some monster stories originate in one place and spread to other parts of the world. Others, like dragon myths, began all at once all over the globe with striking similarities. Where in the world did your favorite monster come from?

Table of Contents

Monster Myths 4
Vampires and Zombies 5
Werewolves and Chupacabras 16
Bigfoot and the Abominable Snowman 18
The Boogeyman 20
Water Monsters and Dragons 22
More Really Weird, True Facts 28
Glossary 30
Index 31
Show What You Know 31
Further Reading 31
About the Author 32

Monster Myths

Monster **myths** often reflect the culture they come from. As the stories are shared, they may travel to new cultures and change over time. Sometimes monster stories are based on things people see but don't understand. Sometimes monster stories are just made up!

Scary Stories

Mary Shelley (1797 – 1851) started writing Frankenstein when she was a teenager. It was published in 1818. The novel inspired movies, and its monster became a superstar of monster lore.

Boris Karloff played Frankenstein's monster in *Frankenstein* (1931) and *Bride of Frankenstein* (1935).

Vampires and Zombies

Vampires may look like you and me, but watch your neck! They're fast, they're fanged, and they feast on human blood. Some disguise themselves as bats. Others become sparkly high school students. Some can be killed with salt, others with silver or stakes. Like all monster myths, the details vary from storyteller to storyteller.

Robert Pattinson as vampire Edward Cullen from the movie Twilight.

Warding Away Vamps

Vampires avoid mirrors, garlic, flowing water, holy symbols, and fire. Another way to disarm a vampire: get them to start counting, then make your escape! Some **legends** say vampires have arithmomania, a compulsion to count everything they see.

The Sesame Street character Count von Count has arithmomania.

5

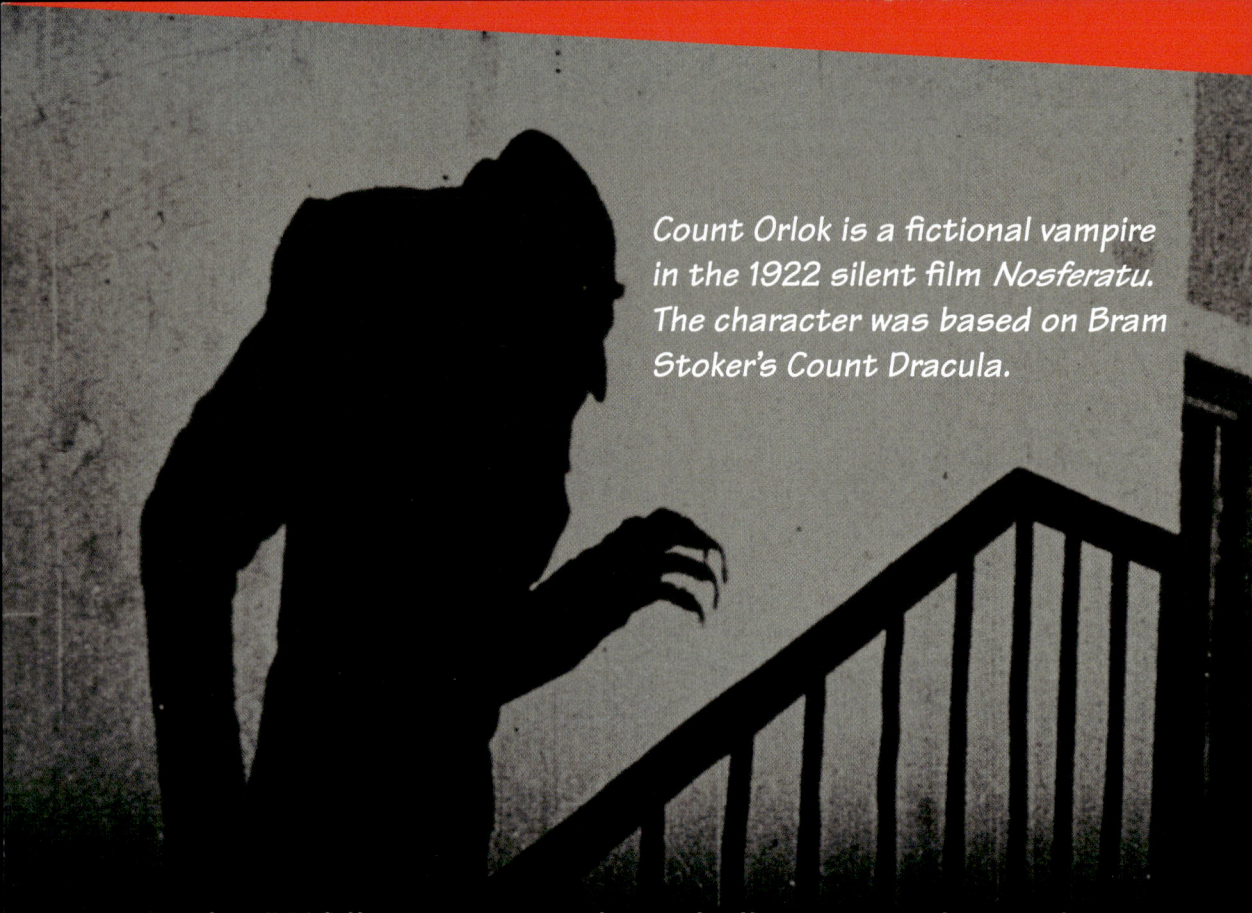

Count Orlok is a fictional vampire in the 1922 silent film Nosferatu. The character was based on Bram Stoker's Count Dracula.

In the Middle Ages, people with illnesses such as rabies, goiter, and the plague were thought to be vampires. A disorder called porphyria caused skin to severely blister in the sun. Some thought its symptoms could be relieved by — you guessed it — drinking blood.

After their death, the bodies of suspected vampires were often decapitated or burned. Others had stakes driven through their hearts. This was done to make sure the person didn't come back to life.

When multiple members of a family died, some people thought their deaths were caused by vampires. The bodies of the dead were dug up to examine for **supernatural** signs.

Have Mercy

A Rhode Island farmer named George lost almost his entire family to tuberculosis in the late 1800s. His community blamed it on vampirism. Each body was dug up and examined. Because his daughter Mercy's body was not decayed, they thought she was the culprit. The townspeople cut out her heart and burned it. The ashes were fed to her sick brother. It was supposed to cure him. He died soon after.

Mercy Brown's gravestone

Author Bram Stoker's Count Dracula character may be the most famous vampire that never lived, but he wasn't the first. Vampires in mythology date back to Ambrogio and Selene, an ancient Greek story of love, jealousy, bloodsucking, and sun sensitivity.

Ambrogio and Selene

According to the myth, Ambrogio fell in love with Selene. The problem? The sun god Apollo had a crush on the human Selene too. Apollo cursed Ambrogio so his skin would burn in sunlight. Ambrogio made a deal with Hades, the god of the underworld. For his part, Ambrogio stole a silver bow from Artemis, the goddess of the hunt. Artemis then cursed him so that silver would burn his skin. But Artemis felt sorry for Ambrogio. She made him immortal. She made him strong. And she gave him fangs. Selene escaped Apollo, and Artemis told Ambrogio how to make her immortal: He had to drink her blood.

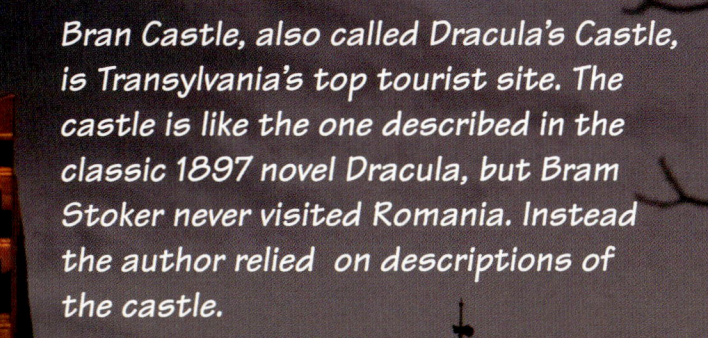

Bran Castle, also called Dracula's Castle, is Transylvania's top tourist site. The castle is like the one described in the classic 1897 novel Dracula, but Bram Stoker never visited Romania. Instead the author relied on descriptions of the castle.

The Real Dracula

Some people think Bram Stoker based Dracula on Vlad Dracula of Transylvania, Romania. Vlad was a cruel ruler who impaled his enemies on wooden stakes. Some stories say he ate his meals among the dying, dipping his bread in their blood.

Vlad Dracula (1431 – 1476) was also known as Vlad the Impaler.

Zombies

They're the walking dead, and they're coming to eat your brains! Zombies are popular pop culture characters, stumbling through books, TV shows, movies, and video games. But the original zombies weren't mind munchers. They were slaves.

The zombie myth comes from 17th century Haiti. African slaves forced to work Haiti's sugar cane plantations lived horrific lives. Death was considered a welcome relief. But they thought anyone who killed themselves became a zombie: an undead slave forced to work the plantations for eternity. To these tortured people, nothing could be worse.

A zombie is usually described as a reanimated corpse or someone bitten by another zombie infected with a zombie virus. They often have rotting flesh.

horsehair

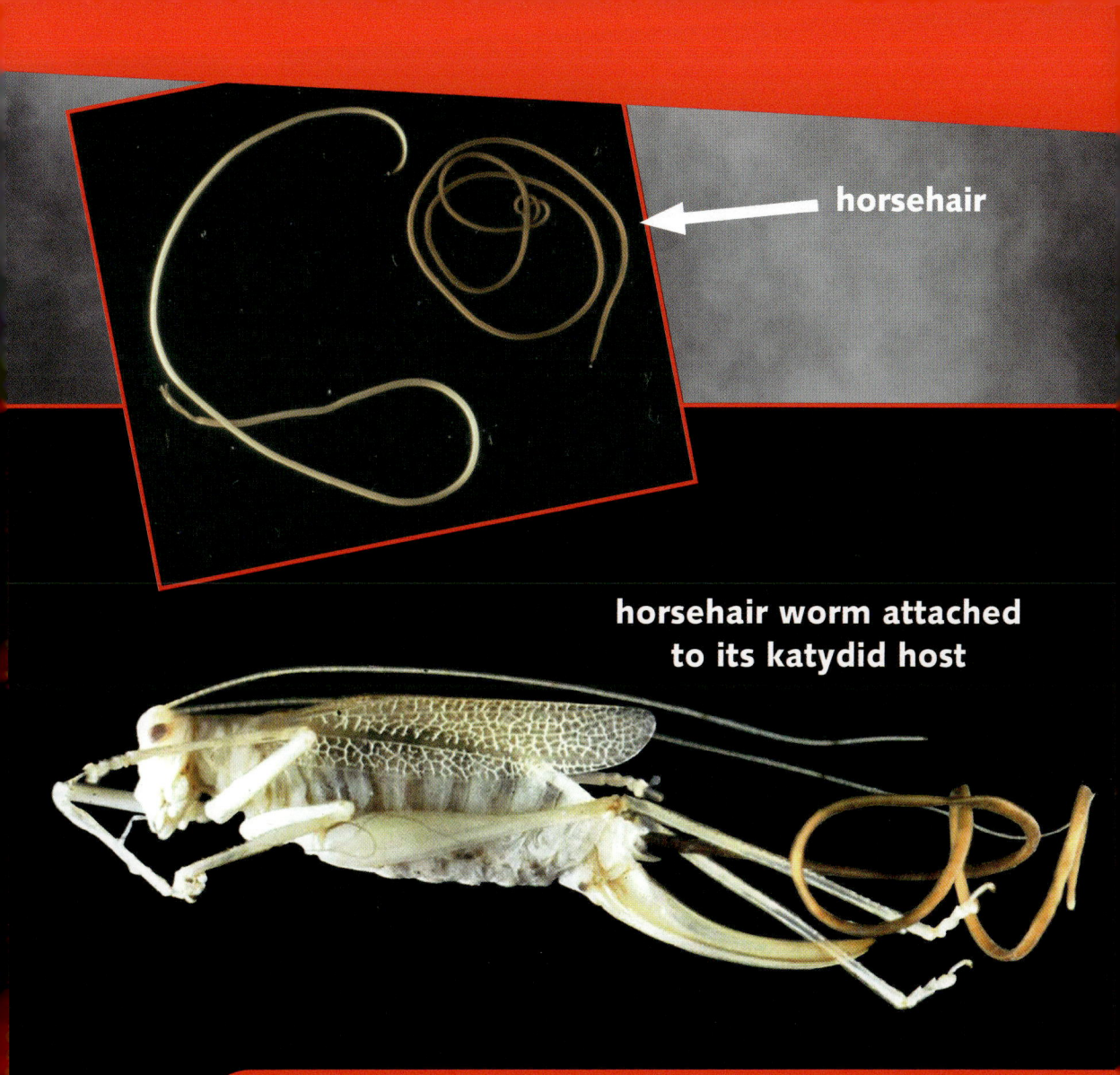

horsehair worm attached to its katydid host

Real Zombies

Some bacteria, viruses, and **parasites** can cause zombie-like traits in their hosts. Horsehair worms get to water by forcing their cricket hosts to drown themselves. Bacteria called phytoplasmas infect plants, sterilize them, and change their flowers to attract insects that will carry the bacteria to other hosts. The plant appears alive, but it's not. It is dead and under the bacteria's control.

Later, a new zombie myth developed and merged with the Voodoo religion. A revolution had set the slaves free, but many feared slavery's return. Haitians thought **sorcerers** called Bokors used zombie powders to bring the dead back as mindless slaves for free labor. The modern image of zombies evolved from this idea of reanimated corpses.

World Zombie Day is an annual event that raises funds for local food banks.

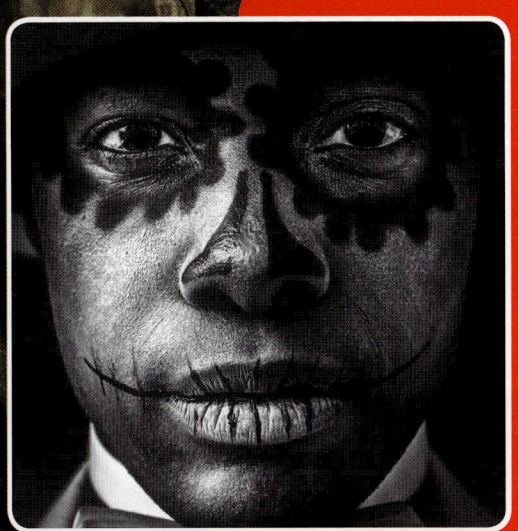

Voodoo

Voodoo, or Vodou, is a religion that originated in Africa. Movies and television shows often make it seem scary. That idea comes from history: Many slaves practiced Voodoo, and slaves were thought to be less than human. Their culture, language, and beliefs were feared by those who would keep them as slaves. Voodoo became taboo. Its priests were labeled witch doctors. Its gods and spirits were called evil.

Werewolves and Chupacabras

Nearly every culture has a werewolf myth — a person cursed to change into a wolf when the moon is full. But in places where there are no wolves, the cursed transform into other predators. In Africa, people transform into lions or leopards.

Some historians think the werewolf myth comes from early hunting practices. A hunter could skin an animal, then wear the skin to get closer to other like animals without startling them. And the transformation from man to animal began! In myths and legends, anyway.

Lon Chaney Jr. played the main character in *The Wolf Man* (1941).

Lions Like Beer?!

One African legend describes a man who became a lion and lived in a hut. His wife brought him food and beer. She also brought the medicine to turn him back into a man.

Chupacabras

In the 1990s, farmers in Puerto Rico found their goats and sheep dead. The animals' necks were mutilated. And their blood was drained from their bodies. Was it a chupacabra? Some thought so. A chupacabra has been described as a cross between a vampire and a big, furry lizard. What could be weirder than that?!

No one has ever caught a chupacabra, but many people have claimed to see them. Their descriptions vary, though. Some eyewitness accounts in newspapers describe the chupacabra as having a "reptilian body, oval head, bulging red eyes, fanged teeth and long, darting tongue." Others described it as ape-like, running on two legs.

Chupacabra means "goat sucker" in Spanish.

As media reports about the incidents in Puerto Rico spread, more chupacabra sightings were reported in the United States and across Latin America. The mythical beast was one of the first to have its legend shared around the world on the Internet.

Many scientists think it's a case of mistaken identity: what people think are chupacabras are really coyotes with severe **mange**.

Bigfoot and the Abominable Snowman

Sasquatch sightings have been reported for more than a hundred years. Also known as Bigfoot, these mythical beasts are rumored to be up to 10 feet (3 meters) tall. But no one's ever caught one. Or found any **remains**. Some Bigfoot believers say that's because sasquatches bury their dead.

One of the earliest Sasquatch stories came from British explorer David Thompson. He found giant footprints in the 1800s. The name "Bigfoot" became popular after a California man was featured in a newspaper with a cast of large footprints he found.

The word sasquatch comes from the Halkomelem word sésquac, which means "wild man."

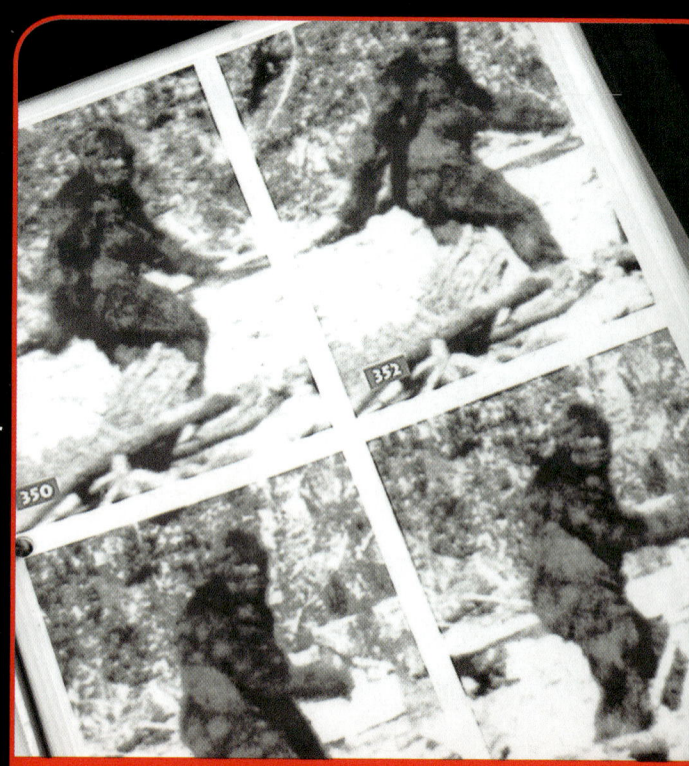

In 1967, Roger Patterson and Bob Gimlin filmed an unidentified subject they claimed was a Bigfoot in Northern California. Since then, many have tried to confirm the footage or prove it was a hoax. None have succeeded either way so far.

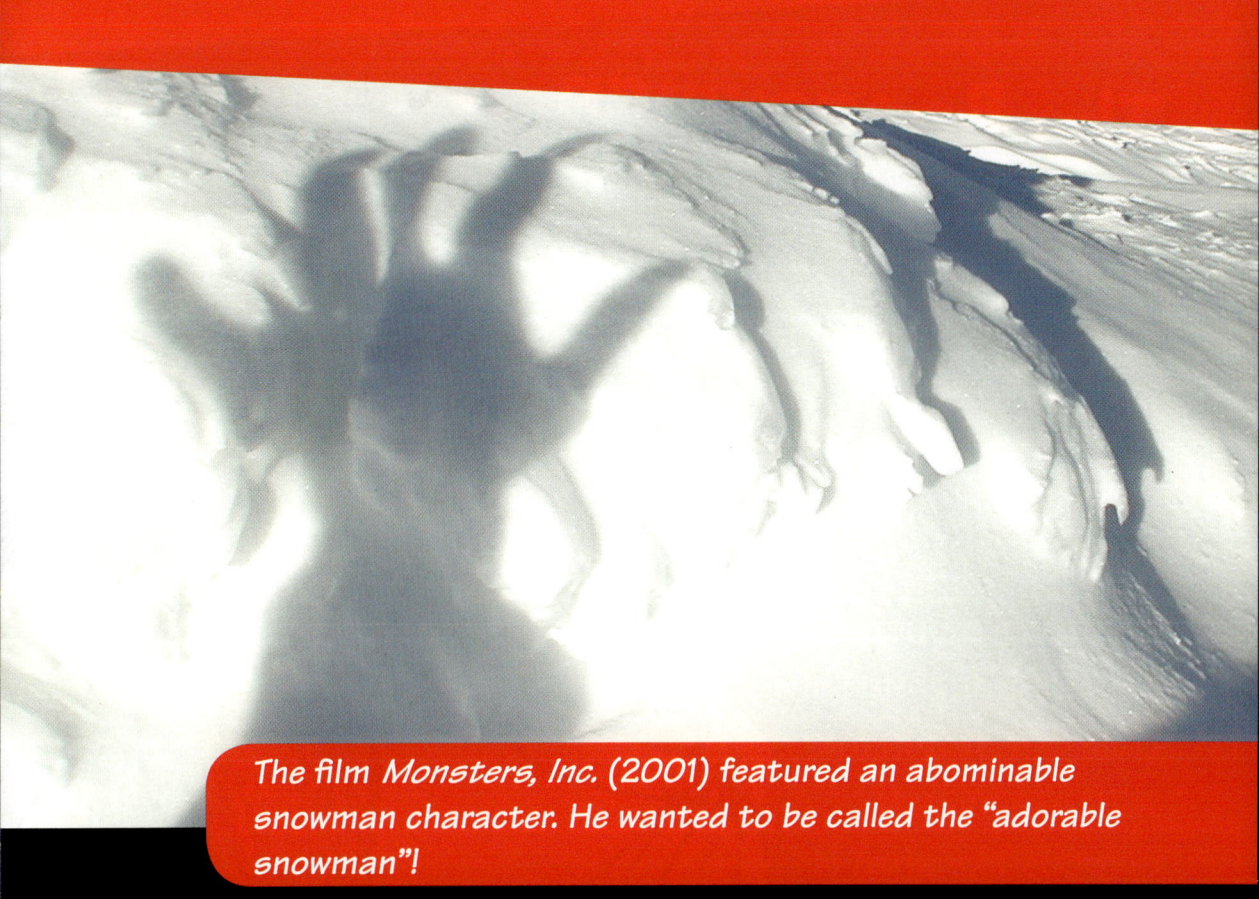

The film *Monsters, Inc.* (2001) featured an abominable snowman character. He wanted to be called the "adorable snowman"!

Like the sasquatch, the yeti is another mysterious giant beast people claim exists. But, like the sasquatch, there's no proof. What's the difference between them, then? The sasquatch is most often spotted in mild or warm climates. The yeti is thought to be a cold-weather creature.

Have you heard of the "abominable snowman"? This term came from a 1921 newspaper report about giant footprints found by participants in the British Mount Everest Reconnaissance Expedition. The newspaper editor mistranslated the term used by the participants. They called it a *man-bear snowman*, but the editor mistranslated it to *filthy snowman*, then changed *filthy* to *abominable*.

The Boogeyman

Nearly every culture has a boogeyman—a terrifying creature that lurks in the shadows, under beds, in closets, or in the woods.

In Australia, the Yara-ma-yha-who is a vampire boogeyman that lives in fig trees, pouncing on people who wander under it. The child-size frogman with red fur and octopus-like arms is said to drain its victim's blood before eating their body. Then it takes a nap! After the nap, the Yara-ma-yha-who pukes up the person—who's still alive. Aboriginal parents used the legend of the Yara-ma-yha-who to warn children not to wander away.

El Coco (also known as El Cucuy or El Cuco) is a boogeyman that eats children who don't obey their parents in Spain and Latin America. Parents warn their children of El Coco with a soothing lullaby:

Sleep my baby,
Sleep, baby, do!
The boogeyman's coming
And he will take you.

Sleep my baby,
Sleep, baby, do!
The boogeyman's coming
And he will eat you.

Black Annis is a boogeyman from English folklore. The creepy hag is said to wander at night, looking for children to eat. Then use their skins for her skirts! Some parents tell their kids Black Annis will get them if they don't behave.

Boogeyman stories vary, but they all have something in common: scaring children!

The word *boogeyman* comes from the Middle English word *bogge*, which means "hobgoblin."

Water Monsters and Dragons

A beast is said to lurk in the waters of Loch Ness, a large lake near Inverness in Scotland. Affectionately called Nessie, the legend of the Loch Ness monster dates back 1,500 years. Despite all the time and the effort put in to finding Nessie, there's still no credible evidence it exists. Divers and miniature submarines searching the lake have turned up nothing. That doesn't squelch monster hunters' enthusiasm, though. Hundreds of thousands of tourists flock to the area to look for Nessie each year.

Some people think Nessie is a myth. Others think it's a living dinosaur. Whatever it is (or isn't), it brings in a lot of moolah! Some estimates say Nessie tourism contributes more than 347 million dollars to

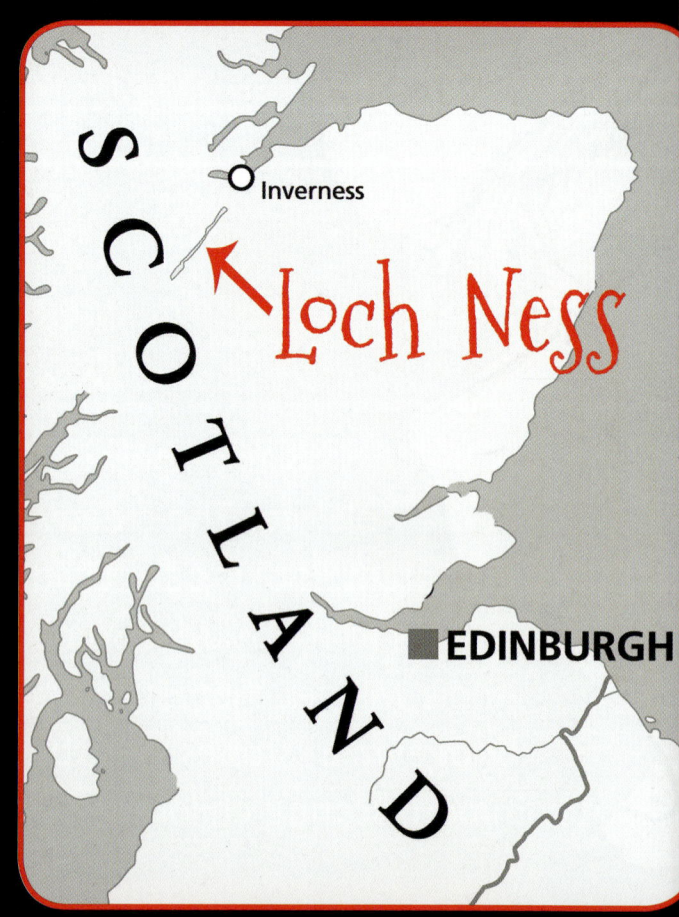

The first Nessie sighting may have happened in 565 CE. According to legend, an Irish monk's servant was attacked by a "water beast" on the River Ness.

Loch Ness isn't the only lake thought to harbor a water monster. Just outside of Fort Worth, Texas, the monster of Lake Worth is said to be a half-goat, half-man that is just as fast on land as in the water. In the late 1960s, hysteria swelled as news headlines told of people who said they were terrorized by the beast.

In Louisiana, the monster of Honey Island Swamp goes way back. American Indians called it the *Letiche*. Local Cajuns call it *Tainted Keitre*. One myth states that chimpanzees escaped from a circus train wreck and bred with alligators, creating the reptilian, web-toed ape beast.

In Canada, the Ogopogo is said to lurk in Lake Okanagan. It's described as a multi-humped monster with a head like a snake, sheep, horse, or alligator, depending on the account. Some people who claimed to have seen it describe it as a log that suddenly came alive.

Lake Okanagan

LAKE MONSTERS of AMERICA

NESSIES
01. "FLATHEAD LAKE MONSTER" – Flathead Lake, Mont.
02. "THE TWILIGHT DRAGON" – Payette Lake, Idaho
03. "ISABELLA" – Bear Lake, Idaho
04. "TESSIE" – Lake Tahoe, California
05. "HAMLET" – Lake Elsinore, California
06. "SKIN FIN" – Lake Powell, Arizona
07. "SMETTY" – Lake De Smet, Wyoming
08. "BLUE DILLY" – Lake Dillon, Colorado
09. "PEPIE" – Lake Pepin, Minnesota
10. "OBOJOKI" – Okoboji Lake, Iowa
11. "ROCKY" – Rock Lake, Wisconsin
12. "LAKE MICHIGAN MONSTER" – Lake Michigan, Michigan
13. "BESSIE" – Lake Erie, Ohio
14. "CHAMP" – Lake Champlain, Vermont
15. "POCO" – Pocomoonshine Lake, Maine
16. "GLOUCESTER SEA SERPENT" – Gloucester Harbor, Mass.
17. "KIPSY" – Hudson River, New York
18. "CHESSIE" – Chesapeake Bay, Maryland
19. "NORMIE" – Lake Norman, NC
20. "ALTAMAHA-HA" – Altamaha River, Georgia
21. "TARPIE" – Lake Tarpon, Florida
22. "MUCK MONSTER" – Lake Worth Lagoon, Florida

GIANT TURTLES
23. "DEEP DIVING TURTLES" – Bottomless Lake, N. Mex.
24. "BEAST OF BUSCO" – Fulks Lake, Indiana

WEBBED HOMINIDS
25. "THE WHITE MONKEY" – Saco River, Maine
26. "TAINTED KEITRE" – Honey Island Swamp, Louisiana

GOAT MAN
27. "LAKE WORTH MONSTER" – Lake Worth, Texas

MONSTER FISH
28. "ILLIE" – Riamna Lake, Alaska

WINGED ALLIGATOR-SNAKE
29. "LAKE CHELAN MONSTER" – Lake Chelan, Washington

HORSE-HEADED ALLIGATOR
30. "NORTH SHORE MONSTER" – Great Salt Lake, Utah

HORNED ALLIGATOR
31. "ALKALI MONSTER" – Alkali Lake, Nebraska

GIANT KILLER OCTOPUS
32. "FRESHWATER OCTOPUS" – Lake Thunderbird, Okla.

HORNED BEAST
33. "WHITEY" – White River, Arkansas

GIANT EEL PIG
34. "HERRY" – Herrington Lake, Kentucky

AQUATIC LYNX MONSTER
35. "MISHEBESHU" – Lake Huron, Michigan

25

Dragons

Unlike some stories that started in one place and spread, scholars think dragon stories developed independently on different continents. And despite the distance and the different languages, the stories were all similar. How did this happen?!

Some researchers point to ancient discoveries of dinosaur bones. People may have found these massive skeletons and thought they were dragons.

Stegosaurus

Others think the reason people everywhere have dragon myths is simple: it's all in our minds! **Anthropologist** David E. Jones said ancient cultures believed in dragons because humans have a natural fear of predators. Early humans were constantly at risk of being eaten by large animals, so this fear became a part of the human mind. This fear was the same in every part of the world. These fears fed the folklore that created the dragon myth, some experts say.

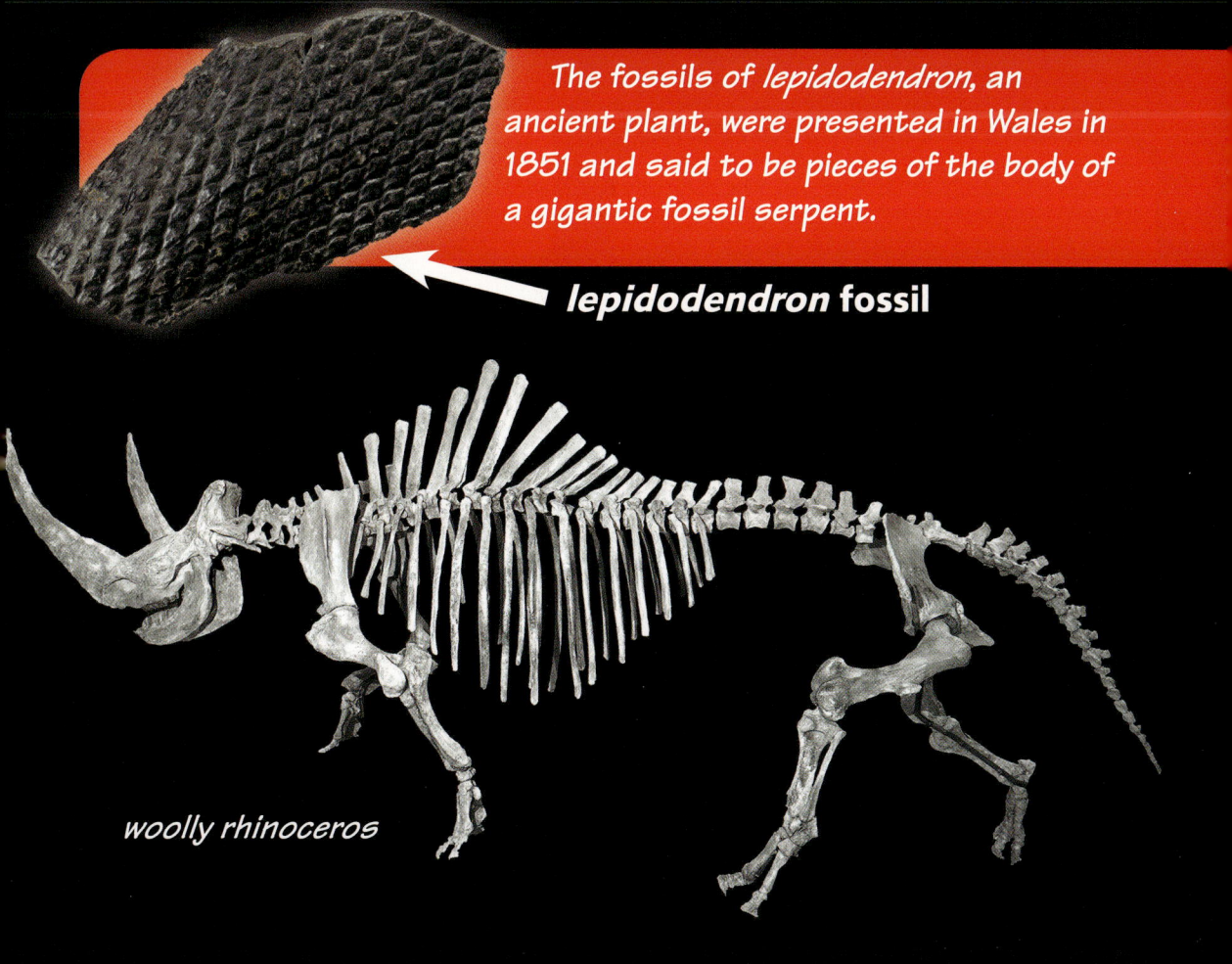

The fossils of *lepidodendron*, an ancient plant, were presented in Wales in 1851 and said to be pieces of the body of a gigantic fossil serpent.

lepidodendron fossil

woolly rhinoceros

27

More Really Weird, True Facts

In Africa, the adze is a vampire that takes the form of a firefly. As an insect, it is said to suck the blood of sleeping humans. If captured, the adze will turn into a human, then eat its captor's organs! A victim of an adze is said to become a witch.

The glawackus is a dog-like beast said to have a cat's face and a blood-curdling scream. It was first reported in Glastonbury, Connecticut in 1939. Newspaper reports tell of hunting parties that searched for the creature. Nothing was ever found.

The snallygaster is part-bird, part-reptile. Legends claim the snallygaster lives in the area around Washington, D.C. and Frederick County, Maryland. During the prohibition period (1920 – 1933), people who made illegal alcohol used the story to explain loud noises coming from their stills and scare others away.

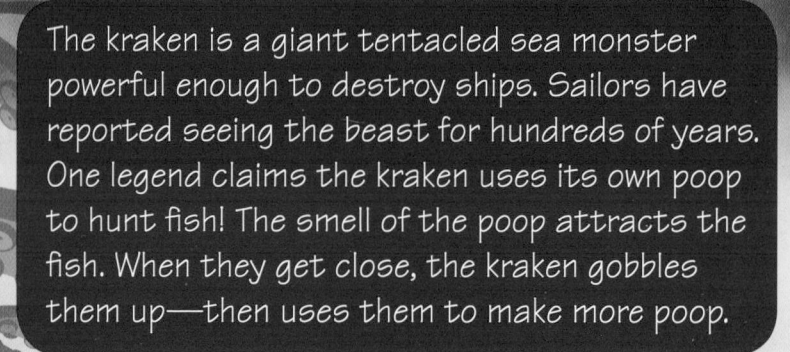

The kraken is a giant tentacled sea monster powerful enough to destroy ships. Sailors have reported seeing the beast for hundreds of years. One legend claims the kraken uses its own poop to hunt fish! The smell of the poop attracts the fish. When they get close, the kraken gobbles them up—then uses them to make more poop.

The Jersey devil, a kangaroo-like creature with dragon-like wings and horns, is said to call New Jersey home. The National Hockey League's New Jersey Devils team is named after this mythical monster.

Boo! Did that scare you? The oldest record of the word *boo* dates from the 18th century. These writings say the word was used in Scotland to scare crying children.

An Australian fable tells of the drop bear, a large, fanged koala that attacks foreign tourists.

Have you heard the phrase "screaming like a banshee"? A banshee is a female spirit from Irish mythology. This monstrous madam is said to foretell a death with her screams.

Glossary

anthropologist (an-thruh-PAH-luh-jist): someone who studies the beliefs and customs of different people and cultures

legends (LEJ-uhnds): stories handed down from earlier times

mange (maynj): a skin disease that causes itching, hair loss, and the formation of scabs and lesions

myths (miths): old stories that reflect the beliefs of a group of people, or explain events

parasites (PAR-uh-sites): animals or plants that live inside another animal or plant

remains (ri-MAYNS): dead body

sorcerers (SOR-sur-ers): people who practice magic by controlling spirits

supernatural (soo-pur-NACH-ur-uhl): existing outside normal human experience or knowledge